NEW WORLD GREETINGS

INSPIRATIONAL POETRY AND MUSINGS FOR A NEW WORLD

Mary McManus

PublishAmerica
Baltimore

First printing

ISBN: 1-4241-9206-4
PUBLISHED BY PUBLISHAMERICA, LLLP
www.publishamerica.com
Baltimore

Printed in the United States of America

Dedication

This book is lovingly dedicated to my husband, Tom, and my twins, Ruth Anne and Tom. Their unconditional love and support helped me to heal.

Acknowledgments

In loving gratitude

To God—our loving Creator without whom this book would not be possible.

To my family whose love and inspiration fueled the creative process.

To my beloved husband Tom for his unwavering belief and constant support and love.

To my twins—Tom and Ruth Anne for teaching me well.

To Ruth Anne for choosing the date I'd leave the VA and for making sure I didn't take myself too seriously.

To Tom for listening to my poems for hours on end and teaching me how to eat vegan.

To the staff at the Post Polio Clinic at Spaulding Framingham— Anna Rubin for taking my hand and supporting me as I made "that first phone call," Dr. Darren Rosenberg, and Kerry Blossfeld, P.T., for helping me take the first steps on this amazing journey.

To Dr. El Abd, a master magician at the Spine Center at Newton Wellesley Hospital and Spaulding Rehab who told me "this is a slam dunk."

To Allison Lamarre, my beloved physical therapist at Spaulding Rehab Boston, for the magical healing and physical transformation you helped birth in me.

And to all the healers who nurtured me,

With deepest gratitude and love to all who I've met along my
journey who helped me to grow and arrive at this moment.

Mary McManus
June 2007

Table of Contents

INTRODUCTION

My story is not unique nor is my past important. Our lives are not about the past or our vision for the future but how we live our lives right now—in this very moment. What **is** unique is the creative process I experienced as I emerged from my cocoon of 48 years to fly freely with God.

I experienced paralytic polio at the age of 5. I had a vision of a "being" in a long flowing white beard inviting me to step into a well bucket. I was reeled up to meet this being. No matter where I looked, I saw this being—in my storybook, on the ceiling. I saw the being whether my eyes were open or closed.

This being—God, Creator, Divine Mind—has always been with me. From inside my safe cocoon I heard the Voice; at times I even listened to the Voice, but never as clearly as I did in January 2007. Many events converged in my life and my soul opened wide to give voice to God's Voice through poetry. Whether I call God She, or He, or Loving Creator, I am referring to the Divine essence and presence in my life; the Divine presence from which we were all given life.

My hope as you read these words is that I can ignite a spark in your soul or fan the flames of life already burning in your heart and soul. May you find inspiration, peace, joy, love, laughter, confusion, tears, reminiscences, reflection…and experience your own uniqueness as you take a journey to a New World.

A NEW DAY

The Gift of Polio

Thank You, God, for the gift of polio which brought me so close to You
While paralyzed I saw Your face no matter what I'd do.
Many wonderful people, You sent them to me at age 5
Perseverance and triumph life's lessons learned but my Spirit could not yet
    thrive.

At age 53 the gift was sent to me a second time,
Having time to sit and feel, to heal I started to rhyme.
The second time more worse than the first yet Your love and wisdom I found
From pain and weakness and fatigue a remarkable Spirit rebound.

Reliving all the trauma of special shoes and such
I discovered so many incredible healers who brought a loving touch.
I had no clue I had such strength and the ability to grow
No matter what the outcome, deep gratitude I show.

And from that place so dark and deep, my body could not move
I took the reins and gained control, this time with nothing to prove.
This gift so precious, I live a new life, gratitude flows from me.
My heart and soul are filled with Grace and each day's a gift from Thee.

Morning Prayer—Dear God

I give thanks to You for this glorious day
I give thanks to You for lighting my way.

For the perfect day ahead for me
Only solutions do I see.

Unlimited thinking is such a gift
Seeing beyond appearances a miraculous shift.

Everyone I meet today I greet with love and care
The blessings which are rich in life with strangers shall I share.

Friendship, family, good health and wealth, You've given all to me
And taught me that in perfect Love only can I be.

A Prayer for Peace

Our loving Creator as I feel You in my soul
I feel only perfection and know I am whole.

If conflicts arise—a new day I'll start
Guided by love You have placed in my heart.

The Light, Love and Truth as my life I live
Flows out to others—if hurt I forgive.

Healing then comes like waves on the sand
Washing away stinging hurts on my soul they can't land.

The Gift

The gift of poetry now in my life
Heals all of the wounds—all of the strife.
Not only for me to the world do I give
Teaching to others this great life we live.

My poems bring a smile, a laugh or a tear
A message live in love instead of in fear.

To gift-wrap up love in a wedding poem
A toast to the couple as they start their new home.

To connect a grieving soul with one who has passed
Preserving their love with a poem that will last.

Poetry described as music for the soul
To help heal this world is my only goal.

Come Out and Play

Arms flung open wide, dancing in the rain
Pure abiding joy to feel alive again.
Healing tears fall and blend in God's puddle
No time to sit in a corner and huddle.

All the old rules driven by fears
Washed away now by God's loving tears.
The imprint Dad left no longer remains
Rain washes away all of the stains.

Baptized with Love, Truth lights my way
The sun shines through on this rainy day.
Splashing and laughing, my heart opens wide
Embracing and flowing, I'm one with the tide.

God takes my hand—release the old way
BATHE IN MY GLORY—COME OUT AND PLAY!

Open Wide the Heart

With God flowing inside, Moses parted the Red Sea
Amazing treasures discovered when I open wide the heart of me.
The hurts and pain of yesteryear now washed away pristine
Allowing healthy tears to flow inside now sparkling clean.
To live a life so filled with joy and love beyond compare
Armour, fears, they melt away, heart now free to share.

A Date with Destiny

Don't wait 'til you die to let your soul fly free
Please listen and hear what happened to me.

My body was broken every imaginable place
Yet to the world—always a smile on my face.

My soul trapped inside feeling it was broken too
God brought me out of darkness "My light I shine on you."

She showed me the way through people I met
It took a while—a message hard to get.

The kingdom of heaven is right inside me
Take the leap of faith—fulfill destiny.

While I did my "soul" work and let it fly free
My body transformed—changes did I see.

My head now aligned—the tremor no more
The strength in my limbs—a stabilized core.

When once head detached from my heart and my soul
They all work together—amazingly whole.

The rules that I live by are only my own
To find strength and courage—my, how I've grown.
I followed my heart to create my bliss
And spread God's word, no greater joy than this.

Take the leap of faith, into Grace I can fall
But I'm floating on air answering God's call.

Don't wait 'til you die to let your soul fly free
There's no reason to live a life in misery.

Follow your passions and I will tell you this
The body falls away healed when you follow your bliss.

The Pinball Machine

Put in the quarters, feel the flippers—I can now take hold

Feeling in control, more valuable than gold.

For many years that little ball bouncing from side to side

Racking up points for others and risking my own hide.

Now I'm the only one who plays—the game of life is MINE

To win I feel my Freedom and let my Spirit SHINE.

The Old Shoe

The old shoe a comfort but it's tattered and worn
It's been on my foot since the day I was born.

No longer it serves me, it now hurts my gait
I walk barefoot with God, my body held straight.

Footprints now left in the still damp wet sand
Alongside the imprint of God's loving Hand.

A Well-Chosen Path

PPS, MS, cancer stroke and more
Many diagnoses exist in the doctor's store.
Does diagnosis shape and a cripple does it make
Or do I use the pain to choose the path I want to take?
No matter what the "outcome" there's no way I can fail
For when I take the hand of God through adversity I can sail.
The body is imperfect but my soul is shining free
There's never any limit to the true essence of me.
I get in tune and get in step knowing every limb is healed
Running wildly with the wind, embracing flowers in the field.
I love myself beyond all words a message says to "live"
And with this overflowing love to others do I give.

Miraculous Machine

Eradicating all disease I use my powerful mind
And gently, lovingly guide myself to perfect health I find.

Steady building muscles become now great and strong
Where once there was a short left leg, it's now gotten long.

While exercising parts of me that had been once diseased
My mind's eye coaxes them along, "With you I am so pleased."

For you're a wondrous great machine, joints oiled with great Love
All work in perfect tandem, fitting snugly as a glove.

The brace I wore upon my leg no longer do I need
And muscle burns, it feels so good, my body it is freed.

The healing, yes, I did a lot but credit it is due
To our marvelous wondrous Creator—dear God, I say,
THANK YOU!

Reflections for Perfect Health

Dedicated to Allison Lamarre, beloved physical therapist

Two arms that once were aching—now so great and strong
To hug and wrap 'round loved ones, right where they belong.

Two legs that were so weakened—now hold the body straight
To walk in beautiful sunshine alongside a loving mate.

A back once curved and wracked with pain now holds the head up high
To see God's glorious paintings spread across the sky.

All feelings of unwellness now replaced with health
Priceless treasure feeling whole, there is no greater wealth.

Gently Rise

Listen to the quiet that surrounds as you awake
Concentrate—be aware of each deep breath you take
Give thanks to God and celebrate—there's so much you can do
A new day's an opportunity to recreate a wonderful you!

As you lie there in the quiet, reflect on all your soul
Trusting that in broken places God does make you whole.
Take your time—be still—and slowly open your eyes
Be gentle with your body as you stretch and rise.

Gaze beyond your room to the beautiful world outside
And remember all the steps you take, your angels, they will guide.

Wake-Up Call

A sound outside the window beckons me awake
Nature's own alarm clock as each deep breath I take
The birds' songs have a rhythm no man could ever write
I feel their precious presence although they're far from sight.

Their songs invite me on this day to live my highest self
Put all thoughts not from God to rest right on the shelf.
As I travel through this day if thoughts should start to drift
Holding birds' songs close to heart, my focus will I shift.

Children of God

It's 5:30 a.m.
I'm gently nudged awake
I grab my pen and paper
More dictation do I take.
This message to the world it seems
I am the chosen one
And we all have this power
Not only God's chosen Son.

The power is a thing called Love
meant for all to share
To treat each other with deep regard
to show all things you care.
Each person is a treasure
Inside you'll find the gem
God speaks to each and every one...
Yes, we're one of them.

The world needs so much healing
Give birth and make a start
Learn to live by listening
To what God planted in our heart.

THE JOY OF BECOMING

Flying Free

I was a fuzzy caterpillar who inched along through life
Always helping others with their daily strife.

I inched and inched and helping hands to others did I give
And did not stop to sit and think how I wanted to live.

Anxious, fearful, did not show to others how I felt
But deep inside I kept myself, with my own things I dealt.

I wrapped myself in a cocoon so quiet and so dark
And something began to flicker—I felt a little spark.

The spark began to grow and grow, the cocoon no longer there
My wings replaced my tiny legs—I can soar through air!

The butterflies inside of me that signaled fear and doubt
Are now my friends and we fly free to bring world's change
about.

Celebrate Me

No matter who is present, grand love inside of me
Overflows to others—only God then will we see.
I hold the Truth inside of me—sometimes a flickering flame
But never can it be blown out, I live only in God's name.

Others doubt the path I take, can't understand "the why"
I act in love and bringing joy I now can freely fly.

The Birth of a Goddess

Always taught to put the needs of others before self
To do and serve and keep my dreams so safely on the shelf.
Forget about my voice so strong or joy that stays inside
Take care instead of others first—my shoulders are so wide.

And then one day it finally hit, this life is too hum-drum
I'm tending to the entire world and now I feel so glum.
My body aches, I feel so old and nothing left to give
Each day is such an effort, is this any way to live?

I listened to my voice inside and it began to swell
I am a gorgeous goddess and the world I have to tell.
I am so whole just being me and love, it fills my soul
To love me first, to fill my tank, the most important goal.

My body is so perfect and my health brims to the top.
My energy is endless and now I never stop.
I dance around with joy and glee, I am so free to move
The gorgeous goddess plans her day with nothing else to prove.

And as this love spills over, it's fuel to light my way
My life is filled with magic—magic moments fill my day.

Our Loving Creator Wants This for Me

Out of the Universe I harness prosperity
Our loving Creator wants this for me.

Healing is mine—my body's in perfect harmony
Our loving Creator wants this for me.

The splendor of God's canvas—my eyes behold the majesty
Our loving Creator wants this for me.

She paints all of nature, the sand and the sea
Our loving Creator wants this for me.

In my corner of the world only let peace and love be
Our loving Creator wants this for me.

With my life in order my branches reach out
Our loving Creator says this is what life's about.

My roots planted firmly, to YOU I reach out
Our loving Creator says this is what life's about.

I reach out to all, sharing love with no doubt
Our loving Creator says this is what life's about.

And one by one with loving hands we reach out
Our loving Creator says this is what life's about.

Using each of our talents, our treasures the Gift
To this broken world we heal every rift.

The Joy of Becoming

When I first got the word I was a mother-to-be
All sorts of emotions stirred up inside of me.

Joy overflowed and yes, there were fears
When they said it was twins, oh, my God, all the tears.

The excitement, the worry, the pregnancy glow
At only two months, I started to show.

So many old wives' tales I started to hear
How would I know when delivery time was near?

Books about twins seemed to line every shelf
My belly so big I could not recognize myself.

Feeling life inside me dissolved all the stress
A mother's knowing replaced every guess

Seeing their faces on their very first day
Knowing that love would always light our way.

When the Children Are the Teachers

Dedicated to my beloved twins, Ruth Anne and Tom, Jr.

As a parent I always thought I should raise my children well
So I taught them their math, how to write, how to spell.
I taught them perfect manners and to eat like a bird
And hoped that they would act upon each and every word.

But the magic and the miracle that's there for all to see
is so many life's lessons THEY HAVE TAUGHT TO ME!

My daughter, she is quite the gal, so filled with love of life
Tenacious, tender, a sense of play she taught me to cope with strife.
My son the vegan, the anarchist, the activist, the scholar
So quiet and so pensive, but at rallies you'll hear him holler.

About the entertainment world, my daughter knew it all
And I would sit and listen and really had a ball.
About healthy nutrition, my son dug in his toes
And now we all eat vegan and shop where my son goes.

But these are all the outer things, there's so much more to say
About a son and daughter who really light the way,

They've taught me patience, joy and love—a love that has no strings
And opened up my heart and mind to soar on angels' wings.
Through their great and wondrous eyes a new world do I see
Through their wit and wisdom, I've found the one true me.

When God entrusts a child into your loving care
Be prepared to have an experience for which you can't prepare.

Birthdays

All wrapped up and filled with peace like a dove
A baby boy—what a gift of great love
A child, a son, he's full of surprise,
Enjoy every moment as he grows before our eyes.

A sweet little girl we now behold
A gift of an angel more precious than gold.
She's utter perfection from her head to her toes
Relish each moment, each day as she grows.

Can we remember the birthday when innocence reigns?
A clean slate without trauma, without any pains.
To be held oh-so-close and cherished by all
Can we hold onto this feeling when once we grow tall?

These feelings of love so pure and so new
Can I feel all that love when I look at you?
For deep down inside us, the treasure remains
And love can now help to transform all those pains.

On that the first birthday, pureness wrapped up so tight
Can now be released to make this world right.

A LITTLE RAIN MUST FALL

When It Rains for Days on End

Cloudy damp mighty winds blow
Where is the sunshine to give that warm glow?

People complaining, despairing, so glum
Forgetting that God is **always** our chum.

The sunshine is there as the night follows day
Faith, it is strengthened when the sun's kept at bay.

The ebb and the flow, so important to life
Hold onto your faith when you "see only strife."

Circumstances deceive for the eye cannot see
The glorious way God wants us to be.

When the sun reappears and Spring bursts into view
God gift-wrapped this day to give it to you.

A Cleansing Rain

Every tree and flower soaking up the rain
But people ask "When shall we see the sun again?"
Meadows, plants, the birds and bees feel the cleansing shower
They all feel the joy inside of God's great healing power.
People see the puddles, cursing wetness and the mud
The trees, they smile deep inside, feel excitement for their bud.
When the sun peers out again from clouds that rush on by
God's dear friend, ROY G. BIV, appears across the sky!

The Gift of Rain

The rain cleansed the earth, making way for new life
Colors burst forth, erasing world's strife.

Rebirth and renewal, God's tools for the way
A most loving gift we can cherish each day.

April Morning

Rain is gone, the sky is clear
Budding trees are now so near.

A chorus of birds serenade my feet
Walking down front stairs to a magnificent aural treat.

I'm sure to look into the sky—streaks of sun and blue
This glorious day created just for me and you.

Yet unseen grass and flowers are ready, poised and set
To give the world the most spectacular Spring that God's created
yet.

See beyond the now brown earth and winter's barren trees
And feel God's love reverberate in the still cool breeze.

An Elixir of Love

Breathing deeply fragrant air
Not from perfumes anywhere
Mix a long spring rain with a newly bloomed rose
Forsythia leaves, She then carefully chose
Azaleas and wildflowers blended with care
Marigolds and green leaves to nothing can compare
It's an elixir of love so Her presence we can "sense"
Wafting through the soul, Her beauty so immense.

SPRINGTIME

Spring

Can you feel the excitement that Spring is in the air?
Kick off your shoes and run outside—dance free without a care.

Spring's now coming, open eyes, awaken to hear bird's song
When focused on the joy and love, nothing can ever go wrong.

But when winter returns don't ever forget the joy you feel this day
For even in the darkest of times, Love always lights the way.

Springtime in Boston

While driving down Comm. Avenue,
eyes behold glorious Spring
Seeing trees and flowers in bloom
heart and soul do sing.

The colors ...white, green, pink
don't know name of flower or tree
Feel the splendor all around
of everything I see.

Where once the frog pond covered in ice
and skaters danced around
Now the grass is
oh-so-green and covers Commons' ground.

Some trees still bare
remind me of the winter that was past
The joy that's in my heart today
Forever shall it last!

The Easter Lily

Six lovely Easter lilies sit proudly on the vine
Half of them with open faces turned toward warm sunshine.

One by one with God's great love, their hearts they open wide
And know the joy there is to life—no need to stay inside.

Last lily left to open—the most special one of all
She spent the most time contemplating answering God's call.

Flow and Grow

The Easter lily once it blooms doesn't close its petals
The butterfly doesn't go in the cocoon, it flies through fields and
meadows.

The grass doesn't grow back into earth, above ground it shall stay
Flow with the forces of nature as you go about your day.

Celebrate Life!

Feel the Joy!

Speak in the one true voice!

Use imagination to soar
Let go and fly free

Grow to be the magnificent person you are meant to be.

Ants and Mosquitoes

Did you ever wonder why God created mosquitoes and ants?
In nature, nothing is left to chance.

Annoying creatures that you want to smack
Messing up the picnic you worked so hard to pack.

But wait—look again—there's a lesson to be learned.
Hold off on using the zapper so they can all be burned.

The ant so tiny—it's done nothing to you,
It's getting the food for the rest of its crew.

The ant colony a marvel—each ant knows its place.
Yet no one's the boss getting into its face.

They forage, patrol, build nests, care for young
On no one ant's shoulder is responsibility hung.

Communication so clear—through antennae they touch
It's the way that they thrive and accomplish so much.

Okay, ants are good, you'll reluctantly say
But the mosquito—annoying—must be sent on its way.

Perhaps its behavior in the mirror we see
A way to behave that's no way to be.

It buzzes around and takes a small bite
And it doesn't like sunshine—it comes in the nite.

The buzzing—so hearken—feel quiet and peace
Preying on others, you now can release.

Feed yourself well on love, joy and light
God's message now clear to do what is right.

When You Step on a Piece of Gum

The moment it happens you feel it—
Your shoe on the ground does it stay
Your momentum is slowed
And now you find you can't rush along your way.

The faster you try—the stickier things get
The anger and frustration seem to "make" that gum set!
You focus on "my shoes are ruined"
You don't take this as a sign
You don't see a simple solution
Instead you curse and whine.

Just find the nearest bench with grass—
Don't focus on the ground
Forget about that piece of gum and take a look around.

See the faces in the world
Greet strangers with a smile
You'll find your feelings will transform
After a very short while.

And open up your heart and soul
To life's little surprise
That guided you to take a break—
See now you can be wise!

And while you're at it, smile wide, for you were quite the ass
To curse a little piece of gum that now sits on the grass.

Kite Flying

Running fast along the beach, she holds my string so tight

What joy there is to flying free—my colors drift from sight

I bob and weave, a bird's-eye view of ocean and of sand

Surfing on the unseen wind, never shall I land

I wish you could come with me—to feel God's breath this way

But know God's magical presence is with you every day

Gone Fishin'

At 5 a.m. the alarm does ring
Still dark outside but my heart does sing.

Round up my rods, my reels and friends
A fishing day—fun that never ends.

Must catch the tide in early morn
Or the bottom of the boat it will be shorn.

No matter what the time of day
We've gathered again to laugh and play.

Trees in Rock Harbor, an amusing sight
Daybreak comes and the sun shines bright.

Hard-boiled eggs ready to eat
Needing our strength so those fish we can beat!

Fish finder goes off—this is the spot
We wait and we wait—the sun's getting hot!

Then somebody yells, "Fish on"
Off we go
The angler with the fish
Goes toe to toe.

Pull up, reel down,
The rhythm we sing
We see it
The fish
Let's boat this thing!

Bass or a blue
a keeper or not
The suspense is high
Keep that line on spot
Don't let it go loose
It will just spit the hook
Oh no, what's happening?
I can't bear to look.

The fish, it is flying
Mate grabs the gaff
The anglers are cheering
We all start to laugh.

Measure the bass
from the tip of its nose
Under the limit
Throw it back 'til it grows.

Whether the cooler is full to the brim
Or empty inside, faces can't be grim
For nothing can beat the laughter this day
Of time spent on the ocean away from the fray.

FEELIN' GOOD

Sunrise on the California Hills

Grey shadows first appear at the break of day
A scattered patch of blue heralds the sun is on its way.
Spotlight cast on palm trees and haciendas now appear
But the royal majesty revealed once the sky is clear.

I see the mountains and the hills made by the Master's hand
The beauty takes my breath away—before God I now stand.
I am a blessed creature, oh, what a gift to live
And all the gifts She gives to me, back to the world I give.

Bermuda in December

Flying out of Logan with snow still on the ground
Transported to a magical place, blue water all around.
Heart shape seen as descent begins
The passengers' faces all melt into grins.

A blast of warm air—step out of the plane
Doesn't matter if there's sun or if there's rain.
The weather in Boston, it's all snow and ice
Feet sink in pink sand—ooh, it feels oh so nice.

Wreaths hang on Front Street, Christmas lights the harbor frame
The quaintness, the charm, stay ever the same.
Shop around in a t-shirt or sit by the pool
Have a rum swizzle, so refreshing and cool.

Usher in New Year's and dance until morn
Bermuda in December makes you glad you were born.

The Magic Show

Turn off the cell phone and go off-line, pack up the car and go
To experience all the splendor of a glorious magic show.
Nothing up the sleeve, a gull appears, it swoops without any strings
A majestic aerial creature, this gull with gracious wings.
Without a pen or marker—an illusion that's really neat
Imprints magically appear on sand of the seagull's tiny feet.
Another feat of magic, the waves roll in and out
This trip to the beach a time to discover what life's really all about.
The peace of mind to calm the soul, troubles wash out with the tide
When you leave this magical place—remember—
the Master Magician's the guide.

The Ocean

She has a life force all her own, a rhythm and a flow
No one tells her how to move—the waters they just know.
The waves that ripple on the sand, a child's pure delight
A father and son stand skipping stones—what a joyous sight.
Beneath the surface another world of creatures great and small
Plankton, coral, a fish array—all there to enthrall.
The majesty—the splendor—a gift for all to share
A gift from our loving Creator—a sign God's always there.

The Artist's Touch

No paint-by-number painting is this glorious summer sky
Once so gray and filled with clouds a winter's day gone by.
Trees now lush with shades of green
No more barren branches can be seen.

Pinks and whites and purples and reds
Awaken from seeds in their slumbering beds.
All of nature comes to life with the stroke of the artist's brush
Singing birds rejoice—the world no longer in winter's hush.

People shedding winter coats wear smiles on their faces
Amazing now to feel the warmth and love shining from God's Graces.
When in the midst of winter, huddled and so cold
Remember God's loving presence, a story to always be told.

Who drew the barren trees and who made the ice and snow
And why must there be winter?
She gently lets us know.
Without a loving contrast, there'd be no way to feel
All our loving God set forth with tenderness and zeal.

The Symphony

The conductor taps the baton gently in the air
A chorus of sweet voices join in from everywhere
Echoing each other across the "Concert Hall"
No sheet music needed for the Great Composer of all.

Passionate chirps to start the new day
Staccato and whole notes, a splendid array
The musicians invisible, tucked in the trees
Heartfelt songs take flight carried by a gentle breeze.
Through the open window, on human souls it lands
Reminding all of love and light sent from Creator's hands.

The Music of Life

Magic and miracles on the hit parade on the radio frequency of love
Out of conflict, peace descends on the wings of the graceful dove.

Spinning love as our lifelong song, all anger melts away
Release those healing tears of loss—the love will always stay.

What a change in us and a change in the world if only love songs
we sing
Just imagine the transformation and the change to the world we'd bring.

Imagine our hearts as a magnet attracting only love and light
Repelling all the hatred, dispelling the darkness of night.

Attracting Grace, our life's blood flows
The river of life, out to the world it goes.

Attracting loving people, we form a chain of love
And see God's affirmation with a rainbow from above.

WORDS OF WISDOM

Only Good News

How many times you get the call, "Bad news I have today"
Bad news could be good news if you head your mind that way.

Someone's ill—a blessing—a chance for them to grow
Or someone now lay dying—joy awaits beyond what we can know.

"I fell down and broke my leg," said with a scowling face
I smile with a quick reply, "It grows stronger in the broken place."

Pessimist or optimist, the choice is yours to make
As for me there's only good news, that's the path I take.

Driving Without Glasses

Life is life like driving without your glasses
on a darkened road at night,
Concentrate intently on what's within your sight.
Don't look back—it's all a blur,
Let headlights guide your way
Trust your intuition to lead you through your day.

Upward Bound

We're all tethered together as we climb the mountain of life
Working together as a loving team, we minimize any strife.

Regardless of wind or rain or snow, the elements we may face
Pulling in the same direction leads us to find the Grace.

Teach and share all knowledge—don't criticize or shame
When hiking up a mountain, there's no room for blame.

Anger, jealousy, competition or doubt
This mountain climb is not about.

If we cut off one person, the risk is great we'll fall
Instead be still and listen—in the wind and hear God's call.

God beckons us to greater heights—a steady hand She'll hold
To give us all life's treasures in packages of gold.

Feel the strength we have within—but not meant to climb alone
Harden not the hearts inside—we're humans not the stone.

What a joy then rushes through—the summit now in sight
No more to live in darkness—bathed in radiant Light.

The Present

Right now is the present and that's where I live
To precious life's moments, my attention I give.

"The past it is over," I say with a sigh
And cheerfully bid it a farewell goodbye.

The future's not here yet, so pull back the rein
And focus attention on the present again.

Heed the Call

I am so grateful
there are so many people
in the world

To be messengers of God

Don't criticize

Keep an open mind

"Oh, I heard that before"

But wait
Listen
It's different

A call to action in a new way

A new twist on an old theme to make the world new
like sunshine after the Spring rain

I stretch my branches upward
and once again

I GROW!

Gratitude

G reet each new day
R adiating joy with
A n attitude of abundance and
T hanks
I magine no limits
T aking your Spirit to heights unknown
U nwavering Faith
D elightful delicious life when we
E xpress effervescent ebullient

G R A T I T U D E!

Prosperity

P ouring out the Spirit
R unning with the wind
O verflowing love
S hines through
P artnering with God
E verlasting life
R eligion's not the answer
I gnite the God within
T ruth lights the way
Y ou have a table prepared before you

PROSPERITY!

Time

Time goes too fast, it goes too slow, we humans often say
But for nature, time is perfect, feel the rhythm of each new day.

I've got to rush, go here and there, there's so much now to do.
STOP SLOW DOWN WAIT TAKE A DEEP BREATH
This one's just for you!

The clocks, they do deceive, yet a slave to them we are
Be still and feel God's love
Life's more meaningful by far.

She'll be your guiding compass, no matter what the task
Settle down and look within, you only need to ask.

Growing Old

Let wrinkles not be on your soul but only on your face
Rejoice that in this hectic world, you now set the pace.
The golden years, you bet they are, though joints may creak and
groan
Your Spirit and your wisdom blossom tho' the years have flown.

The body is a temple to hold your sacred self
Don't let anybody tell you, you belong now on a shelf.
Erase all thoughts of aging, banish them from your mind
Love yourself and keep awake though others may be blind.

Dance the way your Spirit speaks, let love the music be
Remember when you're one with God, you always will be free.

No More Lies

No more lies or manipulative words

Stay connected to the Divine Mind

Be genuine

Stop fighting against the past
Nothing to prove
There was never anything to prove
They did the best they could
Tried to teach God's ways
But all there is to know is
JOY TRUTH LOVE

Banish thoughts based on any other beliefs

Let tears flow
Wash away untruth
No more desperation—panic—jealousy—envy
Let peace descend
See your shining face made new by water
GOD REFLECTED IN YOU

Go into the world
AND SHARE
JOY TRUTH LOVE

Live the truth of who you really are

See the truth in others

A single snapshot never tells the whole story

See beyond the lies and love them.

Annoying Habits

I hate when you do that, we so often say
I love you, you're perfect—a much better way.

So what if he forgets to put the toilet seat down
Magic happens when you turn a smile from a frown.

Leaving wet towels all over the bed
Change that attitude that pops in your head.

Chewing loudly while eating a delicious meal
Those are sounds of enjoyment, not an obnoxious squeal.

The cap off the toothpaste, dishes in the sink
Don't react out of anger, take a minute to think.

Remember that YOU have annoying habits too
Treat others the way you want them to treat you.

Focus on the Wheat

Focus on the wheat instead of on the chaff
When seeing imperfections, feel a smile and laugh!

Remember only good—let all else fade away
Remember only kindness, these are the memories to stay.

If you're allergic to flowers and receive them as a gift
Know the other's intention was to only give you a lift!

If someone hurts your feelings—send them on their way
Pray for them and bless them as you go about your day.

Taking the High Road

What a blessing when we're with friends who get what we're about
We face a little challenge when there are cynics filled with doubt.
But Love within can flow without and wash the doubts away
Regardless of what happens, my highest self shall stay.

A Parking Prayer

Driving in endless circles round and round every block
Stop this futile exercise—it's time now to take stock
Dare to try a different street that might seem out of the way
See where God might lead you as you re-start your day
Not only does this shift of gears, a parking space you'll find
Staying in communion with God brings such peace of mind.

Hug the Road

Sharing in God's inheritance, we're equal, you and I
To truly feel God's glory, the past we bid goodbye.
Beliefs ingrained from yesterday, no purpose do they serve
Harness all the power, take the wheel and ride the curve.
Driving fast, the view so grand, the wind upon our face
Instead of limitations, there's God with loving Grace.

Clean Out the Clutter

Racing thoughts of things to get done and places you must be
Can clutter a mind and blind you to see
A beautiful flower or buds on a tree.

When details of money and such fill your mind
It's time to sit down, get quiet—unwind.

Whenever you feel there's a fight to be fought
Shower yourself with a cleansing thought.

The noise in the world can pierce a loving heart
Please shut it out—it can tear you apart.

Be still and gaze and look inside
Unearth the treasures so deep and wide
The gems that you can no longer hide.

Take out the trash, feel so refreshed
Present to the world your shiniest best.

The Maze of Life

Life is a wonderful maze
The outcome is never in doubt.
The journey through its twists and haze
Is what life is all about.

When you think you're at a "dead end"
You might find a hidden treasure.
Take a turn around the bend
For a surprise that has no measure.

When you're feeling stuck in a trap
It's time to make a move.
Look within to find God's map
To the way to get in life's groove.

Even when no one's in sight
To lend a helping hand,
Look within to feel the Light
The guide to the promised land.

Open your soul, your heart and mind
Embrace the journey each day.
Your only job, your path to find
Bring joy, truth and love on your way.

Keep Awake

Keep awake and you shall see the signs along your way
Stir yourself from a spiritual sleep as you go about your day.

Give thanks, be grateful, remember "seek and ye shall find"
Focus only on the positive—hold greatness in your mind.

Erase what-if's—instead you'll know that you can hold the key
And tell yourself with utter faith "I deserve a great life for me."

Ignore the outer world of noise—feel only love inside
Ask God for all the blessings—your soul just open wide.

And once you're filled right to the brim, all worries melt away
You now shine the light of Love, forever shall it stay.

Healing

Body broken, no end to pain in sight
Focus instead on God's loving Light.

Doctors are scowling, no hope do they see
Find your own path—Live and be Free!

Miracles come in packages great and small
Harness your Faith, feel proud and walk tall.

Don't let anyone tell you about how they doubt
Healing happens from the inside out.

After the winter, the leaves reappear
That power lives inside you—release every fear.

No matter the "outcome," live life this way
You'll feel loving healing as you go through your day.

Show Me What You Don't Know

Reading the Bible and going to Church all in the service of Me
Show Me what you don't know—dare to fly free.

Staying "safe" in a job for all of your life
Even if it costs you your health and your wife

Show Me what you don't know—dare to fly free.

Listen only to others who speak in My name
And profess they're the ones your sinfulness they'll tame

Show Me what you don't know—dare to fly free.

For deep inside you there's a space where I live
Intuition the guidance to you I do give

Show Me what you don't know—dare to fly free.

Shut out all the noise—the clatter others make
Be quiet and still—your hand I shall take

Show Me what you don't know—dare to fly free.

The heights you can soar, you never could guess
It's your choice to create—heaven or mess

Show Me what you don't know—dare to fly free.

I speak to all—not the chosen few
Open heart, mind and soul—it's all waiting for you

Show Me what you don't know—dare to fly free.

All the rules you've been taught no longer apply
Feel for yourself and with Me **you can fly**

Show Me what you don't know—dare to fly free.

I live through YOU—see my signs all around
What do you do when you see a penny on the ground?

Show Me what you don't know—dare to fly free.

In a newborn babe you see My creation
What happens to this once the train leaves the station?

Show Me what you don't know—dare to fly free.

Miracles you think are a rare event
To you and the world so much has been sent

Show Me what you don't know—dare to fly free.

When something "good" happens you say, "There's the grace"
If something bad happens, there's a scowl on my face

Show Me what you don't know—dare to fly free.

I'm always the constant: Joy Truth and Love
And life's not created by Me from above

Show Me what you don't know—dare to fly free.

You have the power—you have the choice
Just quiet yourself and you'll hear My Voice

Show Me what you don't know—dare to fly free.

Listen to others who felt Me inside
They'll help to love you and be your new guide

Show Me what you don't know—dare to fly free.

There are no demands no "Do this for Me"
Dare to live what you don't know and you shall fly free.

LOVE IS THE ANSWER

Healing the Child Within

When the hurt child of the past decides to take hold
She wreaks havoc inside and must gently be told
Her "truths" are untruths—she now needs to grow
A new way of life to her shall you show.

She's a magnet for problems and believes they must be
She reacts to all others—how can she be free?
Whenever a "problem," she must be to blame
And believes she must sit on sidelines of the game.

If she's left unchecked, aches and pains does she bring
She's afraid to stand on her own two feet and sing
A knot in the stomach to prepare for the worst
And doesn't know how to put her needs first.

She tries to control, to feel safe inside
And forgets how to feel a real sense of pride
She seems tough as nails—no one does she let in
To put her needs first, she believes is a sin.

She doesn't see when there's a real gift of grace
Instead sees a problem she now has to face
Her voice was silenced at a very young age
It's time now to write on a brand-new clean page.

The power of prayer and loving new friends
Shines light on the way—peace now descends
A loving embrace and a kiss on the head
Sends the child within to rest on a bed

A bed filled with feathers, comfort and joy
A place she can play with every new toy
Releasing all anger—releasing all fears
And it's now okay to cry healing tears.

Our loving Creator, the great God within
The God who released us from thinking of sin
She wants us so strong, our bodies not frail
Being in tune with Her, we shall never fail.

Strong mind, body, spirit—we're all three in One
Made perfect to shine in the glorious day's sun.

So now take her hand—join together, be strong
The past now erased—sing your new song
Forge a new path and dance a new dance
Hold her and love her and take a new chance.

Knowing you're held by Love and by Grace
Success, health and wealth are all you now face
Gratitude and love now fill every space
And all of life's days are in this new place.

Love Yourself

Self-praise stinks a favorite phrase of parents from days gone by
Half-hearted compliments given "Well, okay, at least you can try."

And children should be seen not heard
Keep your voice silent, don't say a word.

No opinions should you share, but do each thing by rote.
No room to create, you'll play someone else's note.

For years your voice was silenced—it's now your time—breathe free
It's time for you to hug yourself, "I really do love me."

Replace the constant nagging—find your joy and bliss
And live your dreams, your passions—for life was meant for this.

Choose Love

No longer can I rescue and sacrifice my soul
It's been a long time coming—this feeling being whole.

When love is overflowing and it's yes, I want to say
My body lets me know my choice, it is okay.

If I've chosen out of fear—the way things used to be
An ache, a pain, does manifest—a loving reminder to me.

Love Is the Answer

When I love myself and love the world
the world will love me back.
Free of judgments, free of fear
my treasures I can stack.

Once burned, twice shy
Don't be a silly goose
Watch the magic happen
when love, I let it loose.

When someone says a hurtful thing
release it to God— much peace does it bring.
No need to respond—no need to react
just love the person who forgot about tact.

Relationships with all add to
rich tapestry of the day
Create the weave and fabric
along the journey's way.

Assume and presuppose
lead me down a path of pain
God's message is to love someone
over and over again.
I may not like the things they say
or what they choose to do
Regardless of what happens
I choose to say
I LOVE YOU!

Playing Cards

Dedicated to my daughter Ruth Anne

Glorious sunshine, a gentle breeze, playing a game of "Big Two"
Laughing and playing she says to me, "You know I'm better than you."

She wins every game and I start to feel frustration with every loss
I'm almost ready to say, "Let's quit" and the cards I am ready to toss.

When a heart-shaped cloud catches my eye—I stop to pause and feel
God is Love and joy is renewed as I take the cards and deal.

Transform Fear

When things don't "go your way" and you feel a sense of lack
You might get the feeling God stabbed me in the back.

Your nose pressed to a pane of glass, afraid to live your life
Feeling overwhelmed by guilt, and burdened by your strife.

You look to God and shake your fist, "Why do You do this to me?"
"I live in fear and do what's right, why can't You let me be?"

But this is not the way it is—our Creator's filled with love
And God lives deep within you—not a being from above.
God wants you to be filled with joy—your life to be so free
Release the shackles of your past, discover who to be.

The veil of life is drawn away with angels' loving dance
Inviting you to join them, why don't you take a chance?
Believe you are so wonderful—a creative work of art
Chiseled in God's likeness, you're a gift straight from God's heart.

Soul Communication

For soul communication, no cell phone do you need
Signs are all around you—listen and pay heed.

While you're waiting in a line—thoughts are rushing 'round
Quiet down and listen, there's a message in a sound.

While sitting in a traffic jam and stomach's in a knot,
Shift focus from the cars ahead—give thanks for blessings you got.

And when you're talking with a friend and you can't wait to go
Carefully hear the words they speak—there's something you
should know.

Live in the present moment and all, it is revealed
Use soul communication and the world, it can be healed.

Abundant Love

Instead of seeing reasons why you'll push someone away
Look for all the reasons that person makes your day
Do not let your soul shrink back "They'll take too much from me"
The love we have inside us a majestic endless sea.

Re-Giving

Reduce Reuse Recycle—a familiar childhood chant
Let's work to save the planet—an environmentalist's rant

Recycle cans or paper goods, but also share the wealth
Buy, donate a winter coat to preserve a child's health.

When shopping for your brand-new clothes, buy a second set
 and say,
"Take to a homeless women's shelter, I'll make somebody's day."

Remember there's enough for all—so just give half away
Abundance throughout life, you'll have until you're old and gray.

Abundance for All

When driving to a congested town, you look around and say,
However will I ever find a parking space today?!
So you pull into the parking lot to pay a $10 fee
"Why is it that there's not enough, especially for me?"

Next day you drive around and think, "Let me try—let's see what
I can do"
You're quite surprised when someone leaves—there's a parking
space for you.

Each day goes by and you still find belief, it does the trick
But then one day to your dismay, there's not one quite so quick.
You drive around and doubt creeps in, but on the course you stay
And while you drive you hear a song—your message for the day.

You drive around but one more time and much to your surprise
Not one but two big spaces appear before your eyes.

"This is such fun," you tell yourself but then one day you see
"People are pulling into spaces just ahead of me."
You know this is no time to fret, the handwriting's on the wall
Our loving Creator wants us to know there IS abundance for all.

Love Is Divine

Connect but not attach is love of the greatest kind
We each follow our own paths yet connection we shall find.
This is a love that's borne from God, there are no puppet strings
A love like this, no anchor holds, we only have our wings.
Caring love, not control, respect for what we choose
If there's a disagreement, we know we never lose.
No stomping feet, no pouting face can ever serve us well
No right to judge another, this creates a living hell.
This kind of love is everywhere, it starts inside my heart
An endless river flowing from the place I never part.
I walk my path and sing my own song
But in divine love, please come along.

Recipe for a Relationship

Each step in my life a beginning and an end
In communion with God, my life I shall spend.

Gratitude, the fuel as each step I take
No other person's joy am I responsible to make.

When I am with them, I choose who I shall be.
When we look at each other, only God shall we see.

I follow my own rhythm the breath God gave to me
My heart beats for God alone, She wants me to be free.

Trying to change another is like swimming against the tide
Our journey so much more joyful when we're swimming side by side.

I focus on the big picture, not life's little aches and pains
Like the ocean washes on the sand, I flow for spiritual gains.

Distractions from the past or a hurt inside my head
Can only drain my energy and leave me spiritually dead.

Blinders help to focus on my path for my two feet
The path I walk is filled with joy and life is always sweet.

Gently set aside in life what's not for my highest good
Eliminate regrets and doubts—eliminate the "should."

When my center's the shape of perfect love and love flows all around
I'll join my forces to the world and peace will then abound.

WHEN IT'S TIME
TO SAY GOODBYE

When It's Time to Say Goodbye

Why do we hold on so long afraid to say goodbye
Excitement and new adventures await holding faith on high.

Whether it's a dying friend or role we used to play
There's a higher purpose—let God and move out of the way.

The joy we feel, the freedom too, as we flow with life
Riding with the current avoids a lot of strife.

Let the wind take hold of sails, to port we safely find
Release ourselves—untie ourselves—from ties that used to bind.

The Funerals

So many funerals have I seen to bid a loved one goodbye
A common bond—to share the memories—to come together to cry.

Memories of a life well-lived I've woven into a poem
To pay a loving tribute to one whom God called home.
A quivering voice breaks into song as the words I wrote take flight
The love that dwells within my heart pierces the darkness of night.

A person's body may be spent and gone
But their Spirit and their love live on and on.

I continue on my journey feeling their special touch
And give thanks to God for the gift of a person
who will always mean so much.

A Bird's-Eye View of Love

"Come here, my dear, we must build our nest
I know, my love, this is no time to rest.
Let's go and find a perfect place for our brood.
We need a place where we can easily find food.
You stay right here, I'll go and see
The most fabulous nook high up in a tree."

She listens and waits 'til she hears her mate's sign
And flies off to meet him: "Ooh, this place is divine."

Together they build their new home in a flash
No need for down payment, no need for the cash.

Huddled together they weather wind and the rain
And always know that the sun shines again.

They wait for the birth of their new little flock
And being new parents is never a shock.
Their instincts they follow, know just how to be
To nurture their young until it's time to fly free.

They give them a nudge—their wings they can flap
They're off on their own—just like that in a snap!

No empty nest does this couple now face
They fly off together in love and in grace.

Retirement

A portrait of retirement, though retirement age I'm not
I took the leap and now I'm free—ahh, this sun is hot.
I sleep so well and do my work, but only at my pace
I said goodbye to nine-to-five and that crazy daily race.
I get to choose just where and when and feel so worry-free
Time to feel my love of God and create a healthy me.
At first I was afraid, what if this business fails?
With God I only can succeed, Her wind it fills my sails.
Travel, fun, a joyous thrill, now fill my every day
The steps I take, I walk with God, my faith, it lights the way.

The Gift of Peace

Calm the soul, quiet the mind
See what pictures of peace you can find.

A smiling baby being pushed on its way
A tranquil lake on a bright summer's day.

Morning walk at the ocean's shore
That breath of fresh air when you open the door.

The gift of sunlight through your clean windowpane
The gentle sounds you hear in a warm summer's rain.

Walking in nature, leaves crunch 'neath your feet
Hear your favorite song—it's notes oh-so-sweet.

Let these feelings of peace emanate from your soul
Wash away any pain and help you feel whole.

A Nighttime Reflection

Colors of sunset—it's now day's end
Soon into darkness all colors will blend.

Another day closed in the journal of life
Transform all your thoughts and release every strife.

Be quiet and still—reflect on your day
Was there something you said that you didn't want to say?
Whatever went wrong—in thought make it right
Magnify your love with all of God's light.

Set free all your cares for they can't exist
You're perfection to God at the top of the list.
All struggles, all worries, let them all melt away
With the light that signals the end of the day.

CPSIA information can be obtained at www.ICGtesting.com
Printed in the USA
LVOW082011220312

274298LV00001B/269/P